THIS JOURNAL IS DEDICATED TO:

FROM:

"WHEN YOU SEARCH FOR ME, YOU WILL FIND ME; IF YOU SEEK ME WITH ALL YOUR HEART."

JEREMIAH 29:13

PREFACE

Whether you're wanting to deepen an existing relationship with God or have never had one, welcome!

God has been calling you for a long time, but you've been distracted. These thoughts of needing to get your life in order or to 'wait until you need Him', are misconceptions preventing you from a life of purpose. God is far greater than an emergency lifeline in moments of crisis. He knows you, He loves you, and He has a purpose for your life.

Jeremiah 29:11 says,

"For I know the plans I have for you, declares the Lord. Plans to prosper you and not to harm you. Plans to give you a hope and a future."

God can transform your life, and give you a sense of purpose and direction like no one else. All He asks is that you are open to having a relationship with Him. So how does any relationship or friendship flourish? By spending time together.

Take the challenge to set aside the start of each morning for the next 28 days to seek God. This may be 10 minutes or it could be an hour. Just follow the simple devotional prompts.

After 28 days you'll be able to look back and reflect on how God has worked in the different areas of your life.

TO GET STARTED, MIND MAP YOUR IDEAL LIFE BELOW

[WHAT DOES YOUR PERFECT REALITY LOOK LIKE?]

MY IDEAL LIFE

WHAT ARE YOUR HOPES AND DREAMS FOR THE DIFFERENT AREAS OF YOUR LIFE?

FAMILY
[RELATIVES]

RELATIONSHIPS
[ROMANTIC OR FRIENDSHIPS]

CAREER
[WORK/STUDY]

LIFE
[HEALTH/WEALTH]

WRITE DOWN THREE MAJOR CHANGES / BREAKTHROUGHS

YOU NEED GOD TO HELP YOU WORK THROUGH OR TOWARDS

[YOU'LL REFLECT ON THESE IN 28 DAYS TIME]

Romans 12:1–2 [MSG]

"So here's what I want you to do, God helping you: Take your everyday, ordinary life—your sleeping, eating, going-to-work, and walking-around life—and place it before God as an offering. Embracing what God does for you is the best thing you can do for him. Don't become so well-adjusted to your culture that you fit into it without even thinking. Instead, fix your attention on God. You'll be changed from the inside out. Readily recognize what he wants from you, and quickly respond to it. Unlike the culture around you, always dragging you down to its level of immaturity, God brings the best out of you, develops well-formed maturity in you."

DAY 1/28

DATE: / /

THOUGHTS & FEELINGS

WRITE DOWN WHAT IS CURRENTLY ON YOUR MIND / HOW YOU'RE FEELING

E.G. STRESSED ABOUT WORK / THANKFUL FOR FRIENDS

PRAYER

TAKE THOSE THOUGHTS AND FEELINGS TO GOD

GOD PLEASE HELP ME...

THANK YOU GOD FOR...

READING

READ A DEVOTION OR THE BIBLE

WRITE DOWN ANY KEY PRINCIPLES THAT YOU CAN TAKE FROM IT HERE

WRITE DOWN ANY KEY BIBLE VERSES

JOURNAL SPACE

WRITE DOWN ANY OTHER NOTES, THOUGHTS AND IDEAS FROM YOUR READINGS

RANDOM BIBLE VERSE

PRAY AND ASK GOD TO GIVE YOU A VERSE

FLIP TO A RANDOM PAGE IN YOUR BIBLE OR GOOGLE 'BIBLE DICE'

PRAYER REQUESTS

WHAT DO YOU NEED TO ASK GOD FOR TODAY?

"Those who know your name trust in you. For you, Lord, have never forsaken those who seek you."

Psalm 9:10

DAY 2/28

DATE: / /

THOUGHTS & FEELINGS

WRITE DOWN WHAT IS CURRENTLY ON YOUR MIND / HOW YOU'RE FEELING

E.G. STRESSED ABOUT WORK / THANKFUL FOR FRIENDS

PRAYER

TAKE THOSE THOUGHTS AND FEELINGS TO GOD

GOD PLEASE HELP ME...

THANK YOU GOD FOR...

READING

READ A DEVOTION OR THE BIBLE

WRITE DOWN ANY KEY PRINCIPLES THAT YOU CAN TAKE FROM IT HERE

WRITE DOWN ANY KEY BIBLE VERSES

JOURNAL SPACE

WRITE DOWN ANY OTHER NOTES, THOUGHTS AND IDEAS FROM YOUR READINGS

RANDOM BIBLE VERSE

PRAY AND ASK GOD TO GIVE YOU A VERSE

FLIP TO A RANDOM PAGE IN YOUR BIBLE OR GOOGLE 'BIBLE DICE'

PRAYER REQUESTS

WHAT DO YOU NEED TO ASK GOD FOR TODAY?

"And we are confident that He hears us whenever we ask for anything that pleases him. And since we know he hears us when we make our requests, we also know that he will give us what we ask for."

1 John 5:14–15

DAY 3/28

DATE: / /

THOUGHTS & FEELINGS

WRITE DOWN WHAT IS CURRENTLY ON YOUR MIND / HOW YOU'RE FEELING

E.G. STRESSED ABOUT WORK / THANKFUL FOR FRIENDS

PRAYER

TAKE THOSE THOUGHTS AND FEELINGS TO GOD

GOD PLEASE HELP ME...

THANK YOU GOD FOR...

READING

READ A DEVOTION OR THE BIBLE

WRITE DOWN ANY KEY PRINCIPLES THAT YOU CAN TAKE FROM IT HERE

WRITE DOWN ANY KEY BIBLE VERSES

JOURNAL SPACE

WRITE DOWN ANY OTHER NOTES, THOUGHTS AND IDEAS FROM YOUR READING

RANDOM BIBLE VERSE

PRAY AND ASK GOD TO GIVE YOU A VERSE

FLIP TO A RANDOM PAGE IN YOUR BIBLE OR GOOGLE 'BIBLE DICE'

PRAYER REQUESTS

WHAT DO YOU NEED TO ASK GOD FOR TODAY?

"WHEN I AM AFRAID, I WILL TRUST IN YOU. IN GOD, WHOSE WORD I PRAISE, IN GOD I TRUST; I WILL NOT BE AFRAID. WHAT CAN MORTAL MAN DO TO ME?"

PSALM 56:3–4

DAY 4/28

DATE: / /

THOUGHTS & FEELINGS

WRITE DOWN WHAT IS CURRENTLY ON YOUR MIND / HOW YOU'RE FEELING

E.G. STRESSED ABOUT WORK / THANKFUL FOR FRIENDS

PRAYER

TAKE THOSE THOUGHTS AND FEELINGS TO GOD

GOD PLEASE HELP ME...

THANK YOU GOD FOR...

READING

READ A DEVOTION OR THE BIBLE

WRITE DOWN ANY KEY PRINCIPLES THAT YOU CAN TAKE FROM IT HERE

WRITE DOWN ANY KEY BIBLE VERSES

JOURNAL SPACE

WRITE DOWN ANY OTHER NOTES, THOUGHTS AND IDEAS FROM YOUR READINGS

RANDOM BIBLE VERSE

PRAY AND ASK GOD TO GIVE YOU A VERSE

FLIP TO A RANDOM PAGE IN YOUR BIBLE OR GOOGLE 'BIBLE DICE'

PRAYER REQUESTS

WHAT DO YOU NEED TO ASK GOD FOR TODAY?

"BY HIS DIVINE POWER, GOD HAS GIVEN US EVERYTHING WE NEED FOR LIVING A GODLY LIFE. WE HAVE RECEIVED ALL OF THIS BY COMING TO KNOW HIM, THE ONE WHO CALLED US TO HIMSELF BY MEANS OF HIS MARVELOUS GLORY AND EXCELLENCE. AND BECAUSE OF HIS GLORY AND EXCELLENCE, HE HAS GIVEN US GREAT AND PRECIOUS PROMISES. THESE ARE THE PROMISES THAT ENABLE YOU TO SHARE HIS DIVINE NATURE AND ESCAPE THE WORLD'S CORRUPTION CAUSED BY HUMAN DESIRES."

2 PETER 1:3–4

DAY 5/28

DATE: / /

THOUGHTS & FEELINGS

WRITE DOWN WHAT IS CURRENTLY ON YOUR MIND / HOW YOU'RE FEELING

E.G. STRESSED ABOUT WORK / THANKFUL FOR FRIENDS

PRAYER

TAKE THOSE THOUGHTS AND FEELINGS TO GOD

GOD PLEASE HELP ME...

THANK YOU GOD FOR...

READING

READ A DEVOTION OR THE BIBLE

WRITE DOWN ANY KEY PRINCIPLES THAT YOU CAN TAKE FROM IT HERE

WRITE DOWN ANY KEY BIBLE VERSES

JOURNAL SPACE

WRITE DOWN ANY OTHER NOTES, THOUGHTS AND IDEAS FROM YOUR READINGS

RANDOM BIBLE VERSE

PRAY AND ASK GOD TO GIVE YOU A VERSE

FLIP TO A RANDOM PAGE IN YOUR BIBLE OR GOOGLE 'BIBLE DICE'

PRAYER REQUESTS

WHAT DO YOU NEED TO ASK GOD FOR TODAY?

"ABIDE IN ME, AND I IN YOU. AS THE BRANCH CANNOT BEAR FRUIT BY ITSELF, UNLESS IT ABIDES IN THE VINE, NEITHER CAN YOU, UNLESS YOU ABIDE IN ME. I AM THE VINE; YOU ARE THE BRANCHES. WHOEVER ABIDES IN ME AND I IN HIM, HE IT IS THAT BEARS MUCH FRUIT, FOR APART FROM ME YOU CAN DO NOTHING."

JOHN 15:4–5

DAY 6/28

DATE: / /

THOUGHTS & FEELINGS

WRITE DOWN WHAT IS CURRENTLY ON YOUR MIND / HOW YOU'RE FEELING

E.G. STRESSED ABOUT WORK / THANKFUL FOR FRIENDS

PRAYER

TAKE THOSE THOUGHTS AND FEELINGS TO GOD

GOD PLEASE HELP ME...

THANK YOU GOD FOR...

READING

READ A DEVOTION OR THE BIBLE

WRITE DOWN ANY KEY PRINCIPLES THAT YOU CAN TAKE FROM IT HERE

WRITE DOWN ANY KEY BIBLE VERSES

JOURNAL SPACE

WRITE DOWN ANY OTHER NOTES, THOUGHTS AND IDEAS FROM YOUR READINGS

RANDOM BIBLE VERSE

PRAY AND ASK GOD TO GIVE YOU A VERSE

FLIP TO A RANDOM PAGE IN YOUR BIBLE OR GOOGLE 'BIBLE DICE'

PRAYER REQUESTS

WHAT DO YOU NEED TO ASK GOD FOR TODAY?

"Are you tired? Worn out? Burned out on religion? Come to me. Get away with me and you'll recover your life. I'll show you how to take a real rest. Walk with me and work with me—watch how I do it. Learn the unforced rhythms of grace. I won't lay anything heavy or ill-fitting on you. Keep company with me and you'll learn to live freely and lightly."

Matthew 11:28–30

DAY 7/28

DATE: / /

THOUGHTS & FEELINGS

WRITE DOWN WHAT IS CURRENTLY ON YOUR MIND / HOW YOU'RE FEELING

E.G. STRESSED ABOUT WORK / THANKFUL FOR FRIENDS

PRAYER

TAKE THOSE THOUGHTS AND FEELINGS TO GOD

GOD PLEASE HELP ME...

THANK YOU GOD FOR...

READING

READ A DEVOTION OR THE BIBLE

WRITE DOWN ANY KEY PRINCIPLES THAT YOU CAN TAKE FROM IT HERE

WRITE DOWN ANY KEY BIBLE VERSES

JOURNAL SPACE

WRITE DOWN ANY OTHER NOTES, THOUGHTS AND IDEAS FROM YOUR READING

RANDOM BIBLE VERSE

PRAY AND ASK GOD TO GIVE YOU A VERSE

FLIP TO A RANDOM PAGE IN YOUR BIBLE OR GOOGLE 'BIBLE DICE'

PRAYER REQUESTS

WHAT DO YOU NEED TO ASK GOD FOR TODAY?

"And my God will meet all your needs according to the riches of his glory in Christ Jesus."

Philippians 4:19

DAY 8/28

DATE: / /

THOUGHTS & FEELINGS

WRITE DOWN WHAT IS CURRENTLY ON YOUR MIND / HOW YOU'RE FEELING

E.G. STRESSED ABOUT WORK / THANKFUL FOR FRIENDS

PRAYER

TAKE THOSE THOUGHTS AND FEELINGS TO GOD

GOD PLEASE HELP ME...

THANK YOU GOD FOR...

READING

READ A DEVOTION OR THE BIBLE

WRITE DOWN ANY KEY PRINCIPLES THAT YOU CAN TAKE FROM IT HERE

WRITE DOWN ANY KEY BIBLE VERSES

JOURNAL SPACE

WRITE DOWN ANY OTHER NOTES, THOUGHTS AND IDEAS FROM YOUR READINGS

RANDOM BIBLE VERSE

PRAY AND ASK GOD TO GIVE YOU A VERSE

FLIP TO A RANDOM PAGE IN YOUR BIBLE OR GOOGLE 'BIBLE DICE'

PRAYER REQUESTS

WHAT DO YOU NEED TO ASK GOD FOR TODAY?

"LOOK TO THE LORD AND HIS STRENGTH,

SEEK HIS FACE ALWAYS."

PSALM 105:4

DAY 9/28

DATE: / /

THOUGHTS & FEELINGS

WRITE DOWN WHAT IS CURRENTLY ON YOUR MIND / HOW YOU'RE FEELING

E.G. STRESSED ABOUT WORK / THANKFUL FOR FRIENDS

PRAYER

TAKE THOSE THOUGHTS AND FEELINGS TO GOD

GOD PLEASE HELP ME...

THANK YOU GOD FOR...

READING

READ A DEVOTION OR THE BIBLE

WRITE DOWN ANY KEY PRINCIPLES THAT YOU CAN TAKE FROM IT HERE

WRITE DOWN ANY KEY BIBLE VERSES

JOURNAL SPACE

WRITE DOWN ANY OTHER NOTES, THOUGHTS AND IDEAS FROM YOUR READING

RANDOM BIBLE VERSE

PRAY AND ASK GOD TO GIVE YOU A VERSE

FLIP TO A RANDOM PAGE IN YOUR BIBLE OR GOOGLE 'BIBLE DICE'

PRAYER REQUESTS

WHAT DO YOU NEED TO ASK GOD FOR TODAY?

"SEEK GOD WHILE HE'S HERE TO BE FOUND, PRAY TO HIM WHILE HE'S CLOSE AT HAND. LET THE WICKED ABANDON THEIR WAY OF LIFE AND THE EVIL THEIR WAY OF THINKING. LET THEM COME BACK TO GOD, WHO IS MERCIFUL, COME BACK TO OUR GOD, WHO IS LAVISH WITH FORGIVENESS."

ISAIAH 55:6

DAY 10/28

DATE: / /

THOUGHTS & FEELINGS

WRITE DOWN WHAT IS CURRENTLY ON YOUR MIND / HOW YOU'RE FEELING

E.G. STRESSED ABOUT WORK / THANKFUL FOR FRIENDS

PRAYER

TAKE THOSE THOUGHTS AND FEELINGS TO GOD

GOD PLEASE HELP ME...

THANK YOU GOD FOR...

READING

READ A DEVOTION OR THE BIBLE

WRITE DOWN ANY KEY PRINCIPLES THAT YOU CAN TAKE FROM IT HERE

WRITE DOWN ANY KEY BIBLE VERSES

JOURNAL SPACE

WRITE DOWN ANY OTHER NOTES, THOUGHTS AND IDEAS FROM YOUR READINGS

RANDOM BIBLE VERSE

PRAY AND ASK GOD TO GIVE YOU A VERSE

FLIP TO A RANDOM PAGE IN YOUR BIBLE OR GOOGLE 'BIBLE DICE'

PRAYER REQUESTS

WHAT DO YOU NEED TO ASK GOD FOR TODAY?

"Surely God is my salvation; I will trust and not be afraid. The LORD, the LORD himself, is my strength and my defence; he has become my salvation."

Isaiah 12:2

DAY 11/28

DATE: / /

THOUGHTS & FEELINGS

WRITE DOWN WHAT IS CURRENTLY ON YOUR MIND / HOW YOU'RE FEELING

E.G. STRESSED ABOUT WORK / THANKFUL FOR FRIENDS

PRAYER

TAKE THOSE THOUGHTS AND FEELINGS TO GOD

GOD PLEASE HELP ME...

THANK YOU GOD FOR...

READING

READ A DEVOTION OR THE BIBLE

WRITE DOWN ANY KEY PRINCIPLES THAT YOU CAN TAKE FROM IT HERE

WRITE DOWN ANY KEY BIBLE VERSES

JOURNAL SPACE

WRITE DOWN ANY OTHER NOTES, THOUGHTS AND IDEAS FROM YOUR READING:

RANDOM BIBLE VERSE

PRAY AND ASK GOD TO GIVE YOU A VERSE

FLIP TO A RANDOM PAGE IN YOUR BIBLE OR GOOGLE 'BIBLE DICE'

PRAYER REQUESTS

WHAT DO YOU NEED TO ASK GOD FOR TODAY?

"Give thanks in all circumstances,
for this is God's will for you in
Christ Jesus."

1 Thessalonians 5:18

DAY 12/28

DATE: / /

THOUGHTS & FEELINGS

WRITE DOWN WHAT IS CURRENTLY ON YOUR MIND / HOW YOU'RE FEELING

E.G. STRESSED ABOUT WORK / THANKFUL FOR FRIENDS

PRAYER

TAKE THOSE THOUGHTS AND FEELINGS TO GOD

GOD PLEASE HELP ME...

THANK YOU GOD FOR...

READING

READ A DEVOTION OR THE BIBLE

WRITE DOWN ANY KEY PRINCIPLES THAT YOU CAN TAKE FROM IT HERE

WRITE DOWN ANY KEY BIBLE VERSES

JOURNAL SPACE

WRITE DOWN ANY OTHER NOTES, THOUGHTS AND IDEAS FROM YOUR READINGS

RANDOM BIBLE VERSE

PRAY AND ASK GOD TO GIVE YOU A VERSE

FLIP TO A RANDOM PAGE IN YOUR BIBLE OR GOOGLE 'BIBLE DICE'

PRAYER REQUESTS

WHAT DO YOU NEED TO ASK GOD FOR TODAY?

"He will have no fear of bad news;
his heart is steadfast, trusting in
the Lord."

Psalm 112:7

DAY 13/28

DATE: / /

THOUGHTS & FEELINGS

WRITE DOWN WHAT IS CURRENTLY ON YOUR MIND / HOW YOU'RE FEELING

E.G. STRESSED ABOUT WORK / THANKFUL FOR FRIENDS

PRAYER

TAKE THOSE THOUGHTS AND FEELINGS TO GOD

GOD PLEASE HELP ME...

THANK YOU GOD FOR...

READING

READ A DEVOTION OR THE BIBLE

WRITE DOWN ANY KEY PRINCIPLES THAT YOU CAN TAKE FROM IT HERE

WRITE DOWN ANY KEY BIBLE VERSES

JOURNAL SPACE

WRITE DOWN ANY OTHER NOTES, THOUGHTS AND IDEAS FROM YOUR READINGS

RANDOM BIBLE VERSE

PRAY AND ASK GOD TO GIVE YOU A VERSE

FLIP TO A RANDOM PAGE IN YOUR BIBLE OR GOOGLE 'BIBLE DICE'

PRAYER REQUESTS

WHAT DO YOU NEED TO ASK GOD FOR TODAY?

"If any of you lacks wisdom, you should ask God, who gives generously to all without finding fault, and it will be given to you."

James 1:5

DAY 14/28

DATE: / /

THOUGHTS & FEELINGS

WRITE DOWN WHAT IS CURRENTLY ON YOUR MIND / HOW YOU'RE FEELING

E.G. STRESSED ABOUT WORK / THANKFUL FOR FRIENDS

PRAYER

TAKE THOSE THOUGHTS AND FEELINGS TO GOD

GOD PLEASE HELP ME...

THANK YOU GOD FOR...

READING

READ A DEVOTION OR THE BIBLE

WRITE DOWN ANY KEY PRINCIPLES THAT YOU CAN TAKE FROM IT HERE

WRITE DOWN ANY KEY BIBLE VERSES

JOURNAL SPACE

WRITE DOWN ANY OTHER NOTES, THOUGHTS AND IDEAS FROM YOUR READINGS

RANDOM BIBLE VERSE

PRAY AND ASK GOD TO GIVE YOU A VERSE

FLIP TO A RANDOM PAGE IN YOUR BIBLE OR GOOGLE 'BIBLE DICE'

PRAYER REQUESTS

WHAT DO YOU NEED TO ASK GOD FOR TODAY?

"YET I AM ALWAYS WITH YOU; YOU HOLD ME BY MY RIGHT HAND. YOU GUIDE ME WITH YOUR COUNSEL, AND AFTERWARD YOU WILL TAKE ME INTO GLORY."

PSALM 73:23–24

DAY 15/28

DATE: / /

THOUGHTS & FEELINGS

WRITE DOWN WHAT IS CURRENTLY ON YOUR MIND / HOW YOU'RE FEELING

E.G. STRESSED ABOUT WORK / THANKFUL FOR FRIENDS

PRAYER

TAKE THOSE THOUGHTS AND FEELINGS TO GOD

GOD PLEASE HELP ME...

THANK YOU GOD FOR...

READING

READ A DEVOTION OR THE BIBLE

WRITE DOWN ANY KEY PRINCIPLES THAT YOU CAN TAKE FROM IT HERE

WRITE DOWN ANY KEY BIBLE VERSES

JOURNAL SPACE

WRITE DOWN ANY OTHER NOTES, THOUGHTS AND IDEAS FROM YOUR READING

RANDOM BIBLE VERSE

PRAY AND ASK GOD TO GIVE YOU A VERSE

FLIP TO A RANDOM PAGE IN YOUR BIBLE OR GOOGLE 'BIBLE DICE'

PRAYER REQUESTS

WHAT DO YOU NEED TO ASK GOD FOR TODAY?

"Many are the plans in a man's heart,
but it is the Lord's purpose that
prevails."

Proverbs 19:21

DAY 16/28 DATE: / /

THOUGHTS & FEELINGS

WRITE DOWN WHAT IS CURRENTLY ON YOUR MIND / HOW YOU'RE FEELING

E.G. STRESSED ABOUT WORK / THANKFUL FOR FRIENDS

PRAYER

TAKE THOSE THOUGHTS AND FEELINGS TO GOD

GOD PLEASE HELP ME...

THANK YOU GOD FOR...

READING

READ A DEVOTION OR THE BIBLE

WRITE DOWN ANY KEY PRINCIPLES THAT YOU CAN TAKE FROM IT HERE

WRITE DOWN ANY KEY BIBLE VERSES

JOURNAL SPACE

WRITE DOWN ANY OTHER NOTES, THOUGHTS AND IDEAS FROM YOUR READINGS

RANDOM BIBLE VERSE

PRAY AND ASK GOD TO GIVE YOU A VERSE

FLIP TO A RANDOM PAGE IN YOUR BIBLE OR GOOGLE 'BIBLE DICE'

PRAYER REQUESTS

WHAT DO YOU NEED TO ASK GOD FOR TODAY?

"YOUR WORD IS A LAMP TO MY FEET
AND A LIGHT FOR MY PATH."
PSALM 119:105

DAY 17/28

DATE: / /

THOUGHTS & FEELINGS

WRITE DOWN WHAT IS CURRENTLY ON YOUR MIND / HOW YOU'RE FEELING

E.G. STRESSED ABOUT WORK / THANKFUL FOR FRIENDS

PRAYER

TAKE THOSE THOUGHTS AND FEELINGS TO GOD

GOD PLEASE HELP ME...

THANK YOU GOD FOR...

READING

READ A DEVOTION OR THE BIBLE

WRITE DOWN ANY KEY PRINCIPLES THAT YOU CAN TAKE FROM IT HERE

WRITE DOWN ANY KEY BIBLE VERSES

JOURNAL SPACE

WRITE DOWN ANY OTHER NOTES, THOUGHTS AND IDEAS FROM YOUR READING

RANDOM BIBLE VERSE

PRAY AND ASK GOD TO GIVE YOU A VERSE

FLIP TO A RANDOM PAGE IN YOUR BIBLE OR GOOGLE 'BIBLE DICE'

PRAYER REQUESTS

WHAT DO YOU NEED TO ASK GOD FOR TODAY?

"Can all your worries add a single moment to your life? And if worry can't accomplish a little thing like that, what's the use of worrying over bigger things?"

Luke 12:25–26

DAY 18/28 DATE: / /

THOUGHTS & FEELINGS

WRITE DOWN WHAT IS CURRENTLY ON YOUR MIND / HOW YOU'RE FEELING

E.G. STRESSED ABOUT WORK / THANKFUL FOR FRIENDS

PRAYER

TAKE THOSE THOUGHTS AND FEELINGS TO GOD

GOD PLEASE HELP ME...

THANK YOU GOD FOR...

READING

READ A DEVOTION OR THE BIBLE

WRITE DOWN ANY KEY PRINCIPLES THAT YOU CAN TAKE FROM IT HERE

WRITE DOWN ANY KEY BIBLE VERSES

JOURNAL SPACE

WRITE DOWN ANY OTHER NOTES, THOUGHTS AND IDEAS FROM YOUR READINGS

RANDOM BIBLE VERSE

PRAY AND ASK GOD TO GIVE YOU A VERSE

FLIP TO A RANDOM PAGE IN YOUR BIBLE OR GOOGLE 'BIBLE DICE'

PRAYER REQUESTS

WHAT DO YOU NEED TO ASK GOD FOR TODAY?

"I PRAY THAT OUT OF HIS GLORIOUS RICHES HE MAY STRENGTHEN YOU WITH POWER THROUGH HIS SPIRIT IN YOUR INNER BEING, SO THAT CHRIST MAY DWELL IN YOUR HEARTS THROUGH FAITH. AND I PRAY THAT YOU, BEING ROOTED AND ESTABLISHED IN LOVE, MAY HAVE POWER, TOGETHER WITH ALL THE LORD'S HOLY PEOPLE, TO GRASP HOW WIDE AND LONG AND HIGH AND DEEP IS THE LOVE OF CHRIST..."

EPHESIANS 3:16–18

DAY 19/28

DATE: / /

THOUGHTS & FEELINGS

WRITE DOWN WHAT IS CURRENTLY ON YOUR MIND / HOW YOU'RE FEELING

E.G. STRESSED ABOUT WORK / THANKFUL FOR FRIENDS

PRAYER

TAKE THOSE THOUGHTS AND FEELINGS TO GOD

GOD PLEASE HELP ME...

THANK YOU GOD FOR...

READING

READ A DEVOTION OR THE BIBLE

WRITE DOWN ANY KEY PRINCIPLES THAT YOU CAN TAKE FROM IT HERE

WRITE DOWN ANY KEY BIBLE VERSES

JOURNAL SPACE

WRITE DOWN ANY OTHER NOTES, THOUGHTS AND IDEAS FROM YOUR READINGS

RANDOM BIBLE VERSE

PRAY AND ASK GOD TO GIVE YOU A VERSE

FLIP TO A RANDOM PAGE IN YOUR BIBLE OR GOOGLE 'BIBLE DICE'

PRAYER REQUESTS

WHAT DO YOU NEED TO ASK GOD FOR TODAY?

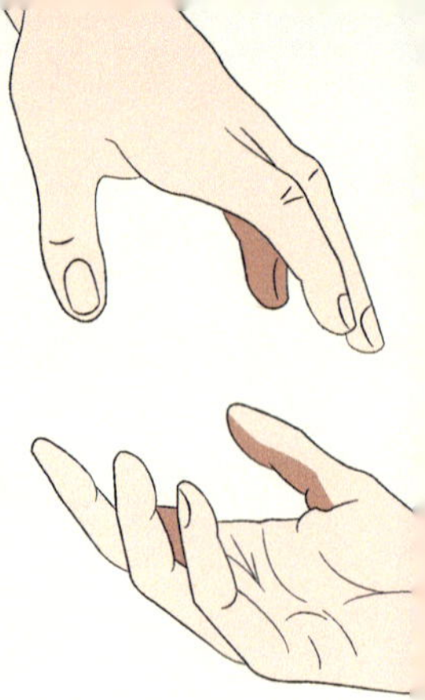

"SO DO NOT FEAR, FOR I AM WITH YOU; DO NOT BE DISMAYED, FOR I AM YOUR GOD. I WILL STRENGTHEN YOU AND HELP YOU; I WILL UPHOLD YOU WITH MY RIGHTEOUS RIGHT HAND."

ISAIAH 41:10

DAY 20/28 DATE: / /

THOUGHTS & FEELINGS

WRITE DOWN WHAT IS CURRENTLY ON YOUR MIND / HOW YOU'RE FEELING

E.G. STRESSED ABOUT WORK / THANKFUL FOR FRIENDS

PRAYER

TAKE THOSE THOUGHTS AND FEELINGS TO GOD

GOD PLEASE HELP ME...

THANK YOU GOD FOR...

READING

READ A DEVOTION OR THE BIBLE

WRITE DOWN ANY KEY PRINCIPLES THAT YOU CAN TAKE FROM IT HERE

WRITE DOWN ANY KEY BIBLE VERSES

JOURNAL SPACE

WRITE DOWN ANY OTHER NOTES, THOUGHTS AND IDEAS FROM YOUR READINGS

RANDOM BIBLE VERSE

PRAY AND ASK GOD TO GIVE YOU A VERSE

FLIP TO A RANDOM PAGE IN YOUR BIBLE OR GOOGLE 'BIBLE DICE'

PRAYER REQUESTS

WHAT DO YOU NEED TO ASK GOD FOR TODAY?

"The Lord himself goes before you and will be with you; he will never leave you nor forsake you. Do not be afraid; do not be discouraged."

Deuteronomy 31:8

DAY 21/28

DATE: / /

THOUGHTS & FEELINGS

WRITE DOWN WHAT IS CURRENTLY ON YOUR MIND / HOW YOU'RE FEELING

E.G. STRESSED ABOUT WORK / THANKFUL FOR FRIENDS

PRAYER

TAKE THOSE THOUGHTS AND FEELINGS TO GOD

GOD PLEASE HELP ME...

THANK YOU GOD FOR...

READING

READ A DEVOTION OR THE BIBLE

WRITE DOWN ANY KEY PRINCIPLES THAT YOU CAN TAKE FROM IT HERE

WRITE DOWN ANY KEY BIBLE VERSES

JOURNAL SPACE

WRITE DOWN ANY OTHER NOTES, THOUGHTS AND IDEAS FROM YOUR READING

RANDOM BIBLE VERSE

PRAY AND ASK GOD TO GIVE YOU A VERSE

FLIP TO A RANDOM PAGE IN YOUR BIBLE OR GOOGLE 'BIBLE DICE'

PRAYER REQUESTS

WHAT DO YOU NEED TO ASK GOD FOR TODAY?

"I HAVE TOLD YOU THESE THINGS, SO THAT IN ME YOU MAY HAVE PEACE. IN THIS WORLD YOU WILL HAVE TROUBLE. BUT TAKE HEART! I HAVE OVERCOME THE WORLD."

JOHN 16:33

DAY 22/28

DATE: / /

THOUGHTS & FEELINGS

WRITE DOWN WHAT IS CURRENTLY ON YOUR MIND / HOW YOU'RE FEELING

E.G. STRESSED ABOUT WORK / THANKFUL FOR FRIENDS

PRAYER

TAKE THOSE THOUGHTS AND FEELINGS TO GOD

GOD PLEASE HELP ME...

THANK YOU GOD FOR...

READING

READ A DEVOTION OR THE BIBLE

WRITE DOWN ANY KEY PRINCIPLES THAT YOU CAN TAKE FROM IT HERE

WRITE DOWN ANY KEY BIBLE VERSES

JOURNAL SPACE

WRITE DOWN ANY OTHER NOTES, THOUGHTS AND IDEAS FROM YOUR READINGS

RANDOM BIBLE VERSE

PRAY AND ASK GOD TO GIVE YOU A VERSE

FLIP TO A RANDOM PAGE IN YOUR BIBLE OR GOOGLE 'BIBLE DICE'

PRAYER REQUESTS

WHAT DO YOU NEED TO ASK GOD FOR TODAY?

"I WILL INSTRUCT YOU AND TEACH YOU IN THE WAY YOU SHOULD GO; I WILL COUNSEL YOU WITH MY LOVING EYE ON YOU."

PSALM 32:8

DAY 23/28 DATE: / /

THOUGHTS & FEELINGS

WRITE DOWN WHAT IS CURRENTLY ON YOUR MIND / HOW YOU'RE FEELING

E.G. STRESSED ABOUT WORK / THANKFUL FOR FRIENDS

PRAYER

TAKE THOSE THOUGHTS AND FEELINGS TO GOD

GOD PLEASE HELP ME...

THANK YOU GOD FOR...

READING

READ A DEVOTION OR THE BIBLE

WRITE DOWN ANY KEY PRINCIPLES THAT YOU CAN TAKE FROM IT HERE

WRITE DOWN ANY KEY BIBLE VERSES

JOURNAL SPACE

WRITE DOWN ANY OTHER NOTES, THOUGHTS AND IDEAS FROM YOUR READINGS

RANDOM BIBLE VERSE

PRAY AND ASK GOD TO GIVE YOU A VERSE

FLIP TO A RANDOM PAGE IN YOUR BIBLE OR GOOGLE 'BIBLE DICE'

PRAYER REQUESTS

WHAT DO YOU NEED TO ASK GOD FOR TODAY?

"THE LORD MAKES FIRM THE STEPS OF THE ONE WHO DELIGHTS IN HIM; THOUGH HE MAY STUMBLE, HE WILL NOT FALL, FOR THE LORD UPHOLDS HIM WITH HIS HAND."

PSALM 37:23–24

DAY 24/28

DATE: / /

THOUGHTS & FEELINGS

WRITE DOWN WHAT IS CURRENTLY ON YOUR MIND / HOW YOU'RE FEELING

E.G. STRESSED ABOUT WORK / THANKFUL FOR FRIENDS

PRAYER

TAKE THOSE THOUGHTS AND FEELINGS TO GOD

GOD PLEASE HELP ME...

THANK YOU GOD FOR...

READING

READ A DEVOTION OR THE BIBLE

WRITE DOWN ANY KEY PRINCIPLES THAT YOU CAN TAKE FROM IT HERE

WRITE DOWN ANY KEY BIBLE VERSES

JOURNAL SPACE

WRITE DOWN ANY OTHER NOTES, THOUGHTS AND IDEAS FROM YOUR READINGS

RANDOM BIBLE VERSE

PRAY AND ASK GOD TO GIVE YOU A VERSE

FLIP TO A RANDOM PAGE IN YOUR BIBLE OR GOOGLE 'BIBLE DICE'

PRAYER REQUESTS

WHAT DO YOU NEED TO ASK GOD FOR TODAY?

"For this God is our God for ever and ever; he will be our guide even to the end."

Psalm 48:14

DAY 25/28 DATE: / /

THOUGHTS & FEELINGS

WRITE DOWN WHAT IS CURRENTLY ON YOUR MIND / HOW YOU'RE FEELING

E.G. STRESSED ABOUT WORK / THANKFUL FOR FRIENDS

PRAYER

TAKE THOSE THOUGHTS AND FEELINGS TO GOD

GOD PLEASE HELP ME...

THANK YOU GOD FOR...

READING

READ A DEVOTION OR THE BIBLE

WRITE DOWN ANY KEY PRINCIPLES THAT YOU CAN TAKE FROM IT HERE

WRITE DOWN ANY KEY BIBLE VERSES

JOURNAL SPACE

WRITE DOWN ANY OTHER NOTES, THOUGHTS AND IDEAS FROM YOUR READINGS

RANDOM BIBLE VERSE

PRAY AND ASK GOD TO GIVE YOU A VERSE

FLIP TO A RANDOM PAGE IN YOUR BIBLE OR GOOGLE 'BIBLE DICE'

PRAYER REQUESTS

WHAT DO YOU NEED TO ASK GOD FOR TODAY?

"BUT THOSE WHO HOPE IN THE LORD WILL RENEW THEIR STRENGTH. THEY WILL SOAR ON WINGS LIKE EAGLES; THEY WILL RUN AND NOT GROW WEARY, THEY WILL WALK AND NOT BE FAINT."

ISAIAH 40:31

DAY 26/28 DATE: / /

THOUGHTS & FEELINGS

WRITE DOWN WHAT IS CURRENTLY ON YOUR MIND / HOW YOU'RE FEELING

E.G. STRESSED ABOUT WORK / THANKFUL FOR FRIENDS

PRAYER

TAKE THOSE THOUGHTS AND FEELINGS TO GOD

GOD PLEASE HELP ME...

THANK YOU GOD FOR...

READING

READ A DEVOTION OR THE BIBLE

WRITE DOWN ANY KEY PRINCIPLES THAT YOU CAN TAKE FROM IT HERE

WRITE DOWN ANY KEY BIBLE VERSES

JOURNAL SPACE

WRITE DOWN ANY OTHER NOTES, THOUGHTS AND IDEAS FROM YOUR READINGS

RANDOM BIBLE VERSE

PRAY AND ASK GOD TO GIVE YOU A VERSE

FLIP TO A RANDOM PAGE IN YOUR BIBLE OR GOOGLE 'BIBLE DICE'

PRAYER REQUESTS

WHAT DO YOU NEED TO ASK GOD FOR TODAY?

"FOR I KNOW THE PLANS I HAVE FOR YOU," DECLARES THE LORD, "PLANS TO PROSPER YOU AND NOT TO HARM YOU, PLANS TO GIVE YOU HOPE AND A FUTURE."

JEREMIAH 29:11

DAY 27/28

DATE: / /

THOUGHTS & FEELINGS

WRITE DOWN WHAT IS CURRENTLY ON YOUR MIND / HOW YOU'RE FEELING

E.G. STRESSED ABOUT WORK / THANKFUL FOR FRIENDS

PRAYER

TAKE THOSE THOUGHTS AND FEELINGS TO GOD

GOD PLEASE HELP ME...

THANK YOU GOD FOR...

READING

READ A DEVOTION OR THE BIBLE

WRITE DOWN ANY KEY PRINCIPLES THAT YOU CAN TAKE FROM IT HERE

WRITE DOWN ANY KEY BIBLE VERSES

JOURNAL SPACE

WRITE DOWN ANY OTHER NOTES, THOUGHTS AND IDEAS FROM YOUR READINGS

RANDOM BIBLE VERSE

PRAY AND ASK GOD TO GIVE YOU A VERSE

FLIP TO A RANDOM PAGE IN YOUR BIBLE OR GOOGLE 'BIBLE DICE'

PRAYER REQUESTS

WHAT DO YOU NEED TO ASK GOD FOR TODAY?

"Do not be anxious about anything, but in every situation, by prayer and petition, with thanksgiving, present your requests to God. And the peace of God, which transcends all understanding, will guard your hearts and your minds in Christ Jesus."

Philippians 4:6–7

DAY 28/28

DATE: / /

THOUGHTS & FEELINGS

WRITE DOWN WHAT IS CURRENTLY ON YOUR MIND / HOW YOU'RE FEELING

E.G. STRESSED ABOUT WORK / THANKFUL FOR FRIENDS

PRAYER

TAKE THOSE THOUGHTS AND FEELINGS TO GOD

GOD PLEASE HELP ME...

THANK YOU GOD FOR...

READING

READ A DEVOTION OR THE BIBLE

WRITE DOWN ANY KEY PRINCIPLES THAT YOU CAN TAKE FROM IT HERE

WRITE DOWN ANY KEY BIBLE VERSES

JOURNAL SPACE

WRITE DOWN ANY OTHER NOTES, THOUGHTS AND IDEAS FROM YOUR READINGS

RANDOM BIBLE VERSE

PRAY AND ASK GOD TO GIVE YOU A VERSE

FLIP TO A RANDOM PAGE IN YOUR BIBLE OR GOOGLE 'BIBLE DICE'

PRAYER REQUESTS

WHAT DO YOU NEED TO ASK GOD FOR TODAY?

"Consider it pure joy, my brothers and sisters, whenever you face trials of many kinds, because you know that the testing of your faith produces perseverance."

James 1:2–3

YOU'VE MADE IT!

CONGRATS! YOU'VE SPENT 28 DAYS WITH GOD.

GO BACK TO THE BEGINNING OF THE JOURNAL AND READ THROUGH YOUR GOALS, DREAMS AND BREAKTHROUGHS.

ONCE YOU'RE DONE, COMPLETE THE GUIDED REFLECTION.

REFLECTION

REFLECT ON THE PAST 28 DAYS. WHAT HAS GOD TAUGHT OR SHOWN YOU?

ARE YOUR DREAMS AND GOALS STILL THE SAME?

HOW HAVE YOU SEEN GOD WORK IN YOUR THREE AREAS OF NEED?

"Give all your worries and cares to God, for he cares about you."

1 Peter 5:7

THE JOURNEY CONTINUES

THE MORE TIME WE SPEND WITH GOD, THE MORE OUR MINDS ARE RENEWED SO THAT WE ARE ABLE TO UNDERSTAND AND OBEY HIS WILL FOR OUR LIVES.

WHEN WE MAKE SPENDING TIME WITH GOD A PRIORITY, HE PROMISES TO TAKE CARE OF ALL OUR NEEDS.

WE CHALLENGE YOU TO SET ASIDE ANOTHER 28 DAYS OF MORNING DEVOTION.

CONTINUE TO USE THIS JOURNAL TO CONNECT WITH GOD. YOU'LL REFLECT ON HIS MIGHTY WORKS AGAIN IN 28 DAYS TIME.

LET'S BEGIN >

GOD WANTS TO MEET US IN THE MIDST OF OUR STRUGGLES. WHAT ARE SOME AREAS OF YOUR LIFE THAT YOU NEED TO ASK GOD FOR DELIVERANCE OR HELP WITH?

MY STRUGGLES

WRITE DOWN THE TOP THREE CHANGES / BREAKTHROUGHS

YOU NEED GOD TO HELP YOU WORK THROUGH OR TOWARDS

[YOU'LL REFLECT ON THESE IN 28 DAYS TIME]

"I pray that God, the source of hope, will fill you completely with joy and peace because you trust in him. Then you will overflow with confident hope through the Power of the Holy Spirit."

Romans 15:13

DAY 1/28 DATE: / /

THOUGHTS & FEELINGS

WRITE DOWN WHAT IS CURRENTLY ON YOUR MIND / HOW YOU'RE FEELING

E.G. STRESSED ABOUT WORK / THANKFUL FOR FRIENDS

PRAYER

TAKE THOSE THOUGHTS AND FEELINGS TO GOD

GOD PLEASE HELP ME...

THANK YOU GOD FOR...

READING

READ A DEVOTION OR THE BIBLE

WRITE DOWN ANY KEY PRINCIPLES THAT YOU CAN TAKE FROM IT HERE

WRITE DOWN ANY KEY BIBLE VERSES

JOURNAL SPACE

WRITE DOWN ANY OTHER NOTES, THOUGHTS AND IDEAS FROM YOUR READING

RANDOM BIBLE VERSE

PRAY AND ASK GOD TO GIVE YOU A VERSE

FLIP TO A RANDOM PAGE IN YOUR BIBLE OR GOOGLE 'BIBLE DICE'

PRAYER REQUESTS

WHAT DO YOU NEED TO ASK GOD FOR TODAY?

"The world and its desires pass away, but whoever does the will of God lives forever."

1 John 2:17

DAY 2/28

DATE: / /

THOUGHTS & FEELINGS

WRITE DOWN WHAT IS CURRENTLY ON YOUR MIND / HOW YOU'RE FEELING

E.G. STRESSED ABOUT WORK / THANKFUL FOR FRIENDS

PRAYER

TAKE THOSE THOUGHTS AND FEELINGS TO GOD

GOD PLEASE HELP ME...

THANK YOU GOD FOR...

READING

READ A DEVOTION OR THE BIBLE

WRITE DOWN ANY KEY PRINCIPLES THAT YOU CAN TAKE FROM IT HERE

WRITE DOWN ANY KEY BIBLE VERSES

JOURNAL SPACE

WRITE DOWN ANY OTHER NOTES, THOUGHTS AND IDEAS FROM YOUR READINGS

RANDOM BIBLE VERSE

PRAY AND ASK GOD TO GIVE YOU A VERSE

FLIP TO A RANDOM PAGE IN YOUR BIBLE OR GOOGLE 'BIBLE DICE'

PRAYER REQUESTS

WHAT DO YOU NEED TO ASK GOD FOR TODAY?

"I can do all things through him who gives me strength."

Philippians 4:13

DAY 3/28

DATE: / /

THOUGHTS & FEELINGS

WRITE DOWN WHAT IS CURRENTLY ON YOUR MIND / HOW YOU'RE FEELING

E.G. STRESSED ABOUT WORK / THANKFUL FOR FRIENDS

PRAYER

TAKE THOSE THOUGHTS AND FEELINGS TO GOD

GOD PLEASE HELP ME...

THANK YOU GOD FOR...

READING

READ A DEVOTION OR THE BIBLE

WRITE DOWN ANY KEY PRINCIPLES THAT YOU CAN TAKE. FROM IT HERE

WRITE DOWN ANY KEY BIBLE VERSES

JOURNAL SPACE

WRITE DOWN ANY OTHER NOTES, THOUGHTS AND IDEAS FROM YOUR READING

RANDOM BIBLE VERSE

PRAY AND ASK GOD TO GIVE YOU A VERSE

FLIP TO A RANDOM PAGE IN YOUR BIBLE OR GOOGLE 'BIBLE DICE'

PRAYER REQUESTS

WHAT DO YOU NEED TO ASK GOD FOR TODAY?

"WHEN YOU GO THROUGH DEEP WATERS, I WILL BE WITH YOU. WHEN YOU GO THROUGH RIVERS OF DIFFICULTY, YOU WILL NOT DROWN. WHEN YOU WALK THROUGH THE FIRE OF OPPRESSION, YOU WILL NOT BE BURNED UP; THE FLAMES WILL NOT CONSUME YOU."

ISAIAH 43:2

DAY 4/28

DATE: / /

THOUGHTS & FEELINGS

WRITE DOWN WHAT IS CURRENTLY ON YOUR MIND / HOW YOU'RE FEELING

E.G. STRESSED ABOUT WORK / THANKFUL FOR FRIENDS

PRAYER

TAKE THOSE THOUGHTS AND FEELINGS TO GOD

GOD PLEASE HELP ME...

THANK YOU GOD FOR...

READING

READ A DEVOTION OR THE BIBLE

WRITE DOWN ANY KEY PRINCIPLES THAT YOU CAN TAKE FROM IT HERE

WRITE DOWN ANY KEY BIBLE VERSES

JOURNAL SPACE

WRITE DOWN ANY OTHER NOTES, THOUGHTS AND IDEAS FROM YOUR READINGS

RANDOM BIBLE VERSE

PRAY AND ASK GOD TO GIVE YOU A VERSE

FLIP TO A RANDOM PAGE IN YOUR BIBLE OR GOOGLE 'BIBLE DICE'

PRAYER REQUESTS

WHAT DO YOU NEED TO ASK GOD FOR TODAY?

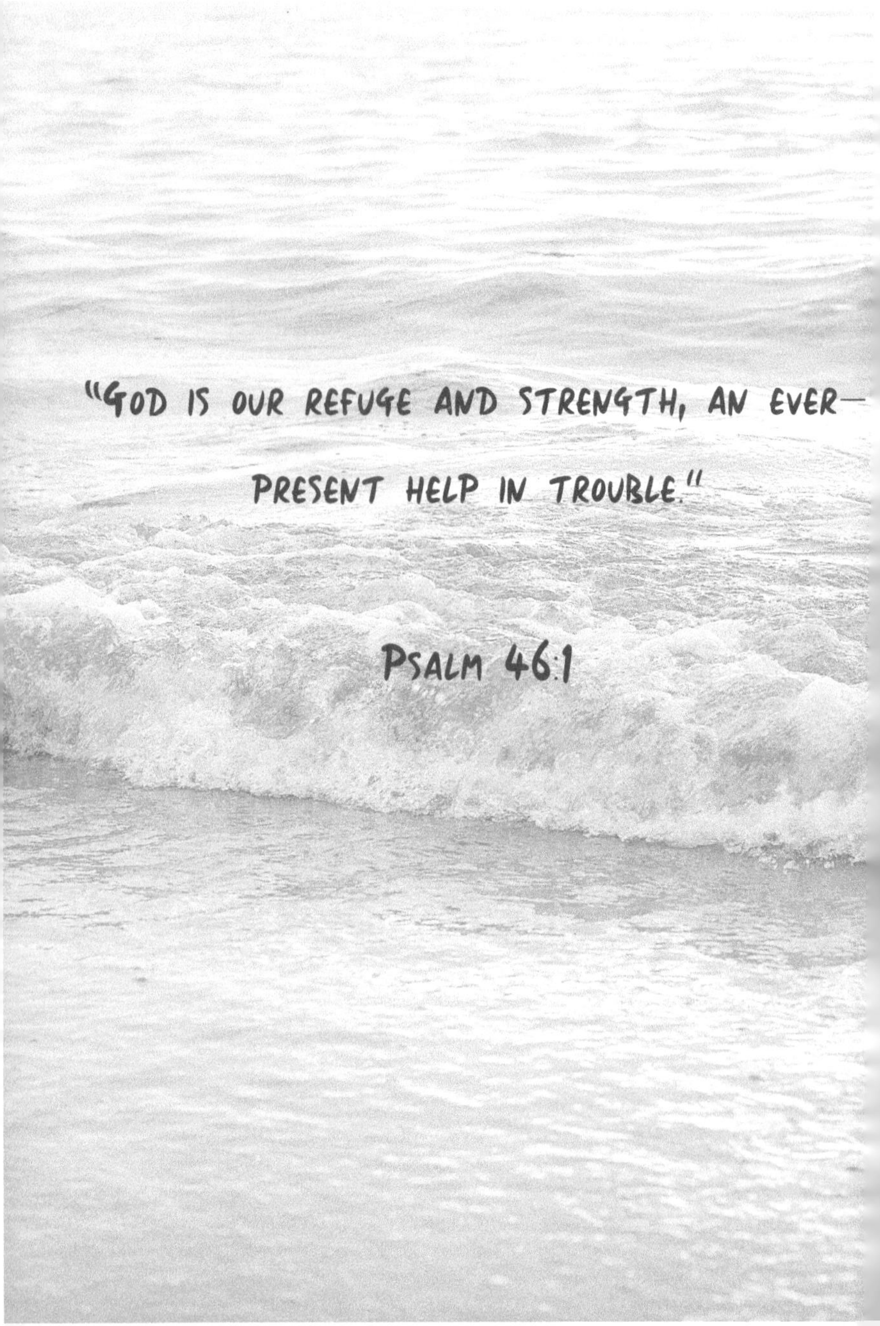
"GOD IS OUR REFUGE AND STRENGTH, AN EVER-PRESENT HELP IN TROUBLE."
Psalm 46:1

DATE: / /

THOUGHTS & FEELINGS

WRITE DOWN WHAT IS CURRENTLY ON YOUR MIND / HOW YOU'RE FEELING

E.G. STRESSED ABOUT WORK / THANKFUL FOR FRIENDS

PRAYER

TAKE THOSE THOUGHTS AND FEELINGS TO GOD

GOD PLEASE HELP ME...

THANK YOU GOD FOR...

READING

READ A DEVOTION OR THE BIBLE

WRITE DOWN ANY KEY PRINCIPLES THAT YOU CAN TAKE FROM IT HERE

WRITE DOWN ANY KEY BIBLE VERSES

JOURNAL SPACE

WRITE DOWN ANY OTHER NOTES, THOUGHTS AND IDEAS FROM YOUR READINGS

RANDOM BIBLE VERSE

PRAY AND ASK GOD TO GIVE YOU A VERSE

FLIP TO A RANDOM PAGE IN YOUR BIBLE OR GOOGLE 'BIBLE DICE'

PRAYER REQUESTS

WHAT DO YOU NEED TO ASK GOD FOR TODAY?

"AND RECEIVE FROM HIM ANYTHING WE ASK, BECAUSE WE KEEP HIS COMMANDS AND DO WHAT PLEASES HIM."

1 JOHN 3:22

DAY 6/28

DATE: / /

THOUGHTS & FEELINGS

WRITE DOWN WHAT IS CURRENTLY ON YOUR MIND / HOW YOU'RE FEELING

E.G. STRESSED ABOUT WORK / THANKFUL FOR FRIENDS

PRAYER

TAKE THOSE THOUGHTS AND FEELINGS TO GOD

GOD PLEASE HELP ME...

THANK YOU GOD FOR...

READING

READ A DEVOTION OR THE BIBLE

WRITE DOWN ANY KEY PRINCIPLES THAT YOU CAN TAKE FROM IT HERE

WRITE DOWN ANY KEY BIBLE VERSES

JOURNAL SPACE

WRITE DOWN ANY OTHER NOTES, THOUGHTS AND IDEAS FROM YOUR READINGS

RANDOM BIBLE VERSE

PRAY AND ASK GOD TO GIVE YOU A VERSE

FLIP TO A RANDOM PAGE IN YOUR BIBLE OR GOOGLE 'BIBLE DICE'

PRAYER REQUESTS

WHAT DO YOU NEED TO ASK GOD FOR TODAY?

"TRUST IN THE LORD WITH ALL YOUR HEART AND LEAN NOT ON YOUR OWN UNDERSTANDING."

PROVERBS 3:5

DAY 7/28 DATE: / /

THOUGHTS & FEELINGS

WRITE DOWN WHAT IS CURRENTLY ON YOUR MIND / HOW YOU'RE FEELING

E.G. STRESSED ABOUT WORK / THANKFUL FOR FRIENDS

PRAYER

TAKE THOSE THOUGHTS AND FEELINGS TO GOD

GOD PLEASE HELP ME...

THANK YOU GOD FOR...

READING

READ A DEVOTION OR THE BIBLE

WRITE DOWN ANY KEY PRINCIPLES THAT YOU CAN TAKE FROM IT HERE

WRITE DOWN ANY KEY BIBLE VERSES

JOURNAL SPACE

WRITE DOWN ANY OTHER NOTES, THOUGHTS AND IDEAS FROM YOUR READINGS

RANDOM BIBLE VERSE

PRAY AND ASK GOD TO GIVE YOU A VERSE

FLIP TO A RANDOM PAGE IN YOUR BIBLE OR GOOGLE 'BIBLE DICE'

PRAYER REQUESTS

WHAT DO YOU NEED TO ASK GOD FOR TODAY?

"THE LORD IS MY STRENGTH AND MY DEFENSE; HE HAS BECOME MY SALVATION. HE IS MY GOD, AND I WILL PRAISE HIM, MY FATHER'S GOD, AND I WILL EXALT HIM."

EXODUS 15:2

DAY 8/28

DATE: / /

THOUGHTS & FEELINGS

WRITE DOWN WHAT IS CURRENTLY ON YOUR MIND / HOW YOU'RE FEELING

E.G. STRESSED ABOUT WORK / THANKFUL FOR FRIENDS

PRAYER

TAKE THOSE THOUGHTS AND FEELINGS TO GOD

GOD PLEASE HELP ME...

THANK YOU GOD FOR...

READING

READ A DEVOTION OR THE BIBLE

WRITE DOWN ANY KEY PRINCIPLES THAT YOU CAN TAKE FROM IT HERE

WRITE DOWN ANY KEY BIBLE VERSES

JOURNAL SPACE

WRITE DOWN ANY OTHER NOTES, THOUGHTS AND IDEAS FROM YOUR READINGS

RANDOM BIBLE VERSE

PRAY AND ASK GOD TO GIVE YOU A VERSE

FLIP TO A RANDOM PAGE IN YOUR BIBLE OR GOOGLE 'BIBLE DICE'

PRAYER REQUESTS

WHAT DO YOU NEED TO ASK GOD FOR TODAY?

"THEREFORE DO NOT WORRY ABOUT TOMORROW, FOR TOMORROW WILL WORRY ABOUT ITSELF. EACH DAY HAS ENOUGH TROUBLE OF ITS OWN."

MATTHEW 6:34

DAY 9/28

DATE: / /

THOUGHTS & FEELINGS

WRITE DOWN WHAT IS CURRENTLY ON YOUR MIND / HOW YOU'RE FEELING

E.G. STRESSED ABOUT WORK / THANKFUL FOR FRIENDS

PRAYER

TAKE THOSE THOUGHTS AND FEELINGS TO GOD

GOD PLEASE HELP ME...

THANK YOU GOD FOR...

READING

READ A DEVOTION OR THE BIBLE

WRITE DOWN ANY KEY PRINCIPLES THAT YOU CAN TAKE FROM IT HERE

WRITE DOWN ANY KEY BIBLE VERSES

JOURNAL SPACE

WRITE DOWN ANY OTHER NOTES, THOUGHTS AND IDEAS FROM YOUR READING

RANDOM BIBLE VERSE

PRAY AND ASK GOD TO GIVE YOU A VERSE

FLIP TO A RANDOM PAGE IN YOUR BIBLE OR GOOGLE 'BIBLE DICE'

PRAYER REQUESTS

WHAT DO YOU NEED TO ASK GOD FOR TODAY?

"AND WE KNOW THAT IN ALL THINGS GOD WORKS FOR THE GOOD OF THOSE WHO LOVE HIM, WHO HAVE BEEN CALLED ACCORDING TO HIS PURPOSE."

ROMANS 8:28

DAY 10/28

DATE: / /

THOUGHTS & FEELINGS

WRITE DOWN WHAT IS CURRENTLY ON YOUR MIND / HOW YOU'RE FEELING

E.G. STRESSED ABOUT WORK / THANKFUL FOR FRIENDS

PRAYER

TAKE THOSE THOUGHTS AND FEELINGS TO GOD

GOD PLEASE HELP ME...

THANK YOU GOD FOR...

READING

READ A DEVOTION OR THE BIBLE

WRITE DOWN ANY KEY PRINCIPLES THAT YOU CAN TAKE FROM IT HERE

WRITE DOWN ANY KEY BIBLE VERSES

JOURNAL SPACE

WRITE DOWN ANY OTHER NOTES, THOUGHTS AND IDEAS FROM YOUR READINGS

RANDOM BIBLE VERSE

PRAY AND ASK GOD TO GIVE YOU A VERSE

FLIP TO A RANDOM PAGE IN YOUR BIBLE OR GOOGLE 'BIBLE DICE'

PRAYER REQUESTS

WHAT DO YOU NEED TO ASK GOD FOR TODAY?

"FOR IT IS BY GRACE YOU HAVE BEEN SAVED, THROUGH FAITH — AND THIS NOT FROM YOURSELVES, IT IS THE GIFT OF GOD."

EPHESIANS 2:8

DAY 11/28

DATE: / /

THOUGHTS & FEELINGS

WRITE DOWN WHAT IS CURRENTLY ON YOUR MIND / HOW YOU'RE FEELING

E.G. STRESSED ABOUT WORK / THANKFUL FOR FRIENDS

PRAYER

TAKE THOSE THOUGHTS AND FEELINGS TO GOD

GOD PLEASE HELP ME...

THANK YOU GOD FOR...

READING

READ A DEVOTION OR THE BIBLE

WRITE DOWN ANY KEY PRINCIPLES THAT YOU CAN TAKE FROM IT HERE

WRITE DOWN ANY KEY BIBLE VERSES

JOURNAL SPACE

WRITE DOWN ANY OTHER NOTES, THOUGHTS AND IDEAS FROM YOUR READING

RANDOM BIBLE VERSE

PRAY AND ASK GOD TO GIVE YOU A VERSE

FLIP TO A RANDOM PAGE IN YOUR BIBLE OR GOOGLE 'BIBLE DICE'

PRAYER REQUESTS

WHAT DO YOU NEED TO ASK GOD FOR TODAY?

"LET THE PEACE OF CHRIST RULE IN YOUR HEARTS, SINCE AS MEMBERS OF ONE BODY YOU WERE CALLED TO PEACE, AND BE THANKFUL."

COLOSSIANS 3:15

DAY 12/28

DATE: / /

THOUGHTS & FEELINGS

WRITE DOWN WHAT IS CURRENTLY ON YOUR MIND / HOW YOU'RE FEELING

E.G. STRESSED ABOUT WORK / THANKFUL FOR FRIENDS

PRAYER

TAKE THOSE THOUGHTS AND FEELINGS TO GOD

GOD PLEASE HELP ME...

THANK YOU GOD FOR...

READING

READ A DEVOTION OR THE BIBLE

WRITE DOWN ANY KEY PRINCIPLES THAT YOU CAN TAKE FROM IT HERE

WRITE DOWN ANY KEY BIBLE VERSES

JOURNAL SPACE

WRITE DOWN ANY OTHER NOTES, THOUGHTS AND IDEAS FROM YOUR READINGS

RANDOM BIBLE VERSE

PRAY AND ASK GOD TO GIVE YOU A VERSE

FLIP TO A RANDOM PAGE IN YOUR BIBLE OR GOOGLE 'BIBLE DICE'

PRAYER REQUESTS

WHAT DO YOU NEED TO ASK GOD FOR TODAY?

"BE ON GUARD; STAND FIRM IN THE FAITH; BE COURAGEOUS; BE STRONG."

1 CORINTHIANS 16:13

DAY 13/28

DATE: / /

THOUGHTS & FEELINGS

WRITE DOWN WHAT IS CURRENTLY ON YOUR MIND / HOW YOU'RE FEELING

E.G. STRESSED ABOUT WORK / THANKFUL FOR FRIENDS

PRAYER

TAKE THOSE THOUGHTS AND FEELINGS TO GOD

GOD PLEASE HELP ME...

THANK YOU GOD FOR...

READING

READ A DEVOTION OR THE BIBLE

WRITE DOWN ANY KEY PRINCIPLES THAT YOU CAN TAKE FROM IT HERE

WRITE DOWN ANY KEY BIBLE VERSES

JOURNAL SPACE

WRITE DOWN ANY OTHER NOTES, THOUGHTS AND IDEAS FROM YOUR READINGS

RANDOM BIBLE VERSE

PRAY AND ASK GOD TO GIVE YOU A VERSE

FLIP TO A RANDOM PAGE IN YOUR BIBLE OR GOOGLE 'BIBLE DICE'

PRAYER REQUESTS

WHAT DO YOU NEED TO ASK GOD FOR TODAY?

"Strengthen the feeble hands, steady the knees that give way; say to those with fearful hearts, "Be strong, do not fear; your God will come, he will come with vengeance with divine retribution he will come to save you."

Isaiah 35:3–4

DAY 14/28

DATE: / /

THOUGHTS & FEELINGS

WRITE DOWN WHAT IS CURRENTLY ON YOUR MIND / HOW YOU'RE FEELING

E.G. STRESSED ABOUT WORK / THANKFUL FOR FRIENDS

PRAYER

TAKE THOSE THOUGHTS AND FEELINGS TO GOD

GOD PLEASE HELP ME...

THANK YOU GOD FOR...

READING

READ A DEVOTION OR THE BIBLE

WRITE DOWN ANY KEY PRINCIPLES THAT YOU CAN TAKE FROM IT HERE

WRITE DOWN ANY KEY BIBLE VERSES

JOURNAL SPACE

WRITE DOWN ANY OTHER NOTES, THOUGHTS AND IDEAS FROM YOUR READINGS

RANDOM BIBLE VERSE

PRAY AND ASK GOD TO GIVE YOU A VERSE

FLIP TO A RANDOM PAGE IN YOUR BIBLE OR GOOGLE 'BIBLE DICE'

PRAYER REQUESTS

WHAT DO YOU NEED TO ASK GOD FOR TODAY?

"THE LORD IS GOOD TO ALL; HE HAS COMPASSION ON ALL HE HAS MADE."

PSALM 145:9

DAY 15/28

DATE: / /

THOUGHTS & FEELINGS

WRITE DOWN WHAT IS CURRENTLY ON YOUR MIND / HOW YOU'RE FEELING

E.G. STRESSED ABOUT WORK / THANKFUL FOR FRIENDS

PRAYER

TAKE THOSE THOUGHTS AND FEELINGS TO GOD

GOD PLEASE HELP ME...

THANK YOU GOD FOR...

READING

READ A DEVOTION OR THE BIBLE

WRITE DOWN ANY KEY PRINCIPLES THAT YOU CAN TAKE FROM IT HERE

WRITE DOWN ANY KEY BIBLE VERSES

JOURNAL SPACE

WRITE DOWN ANY OTHER NOTES, THOUGHTS AND IDEAS FROM YOUR READING

RANDOM BIBLE VERSE

PRAY AND ASK GOD TO GIVE YOU A VERSE

FLIP TO A RANDOM PAGE IN YOUR BIBLE OR GOOGLE 'BIBLE DICE'

PRAYER REQUESTS

WHAT DO YOU NEED TO ASK GOD FOR TODAY?

"Have I not commanded you? Be strong and courageous. Do not be afraid; do not be discouraged, for the Lord your God will be with you wherever you go."

Joshua 1:9

DAY 16/28

DATE: / /

THOUGHTS & FEELINGS

WRITE DOWN WHAT IS CURRENTLY ON YOUR MIND / HOW YOU'RE FEELING

E.G. STRESSED ABOUT WORK / THANKFUL FOR FRIENDS

PRAYER

TAKE THOSE THOUGHTS AND FEELINGS TO GOD

GOD PLEASE HELP ME...

THANK YOU GOD FOR...

READING

READ A DEVOTION OR THE BIBLE

WRITE DOWN ANY KEY PRINCIPLES THAT YOU CAN TAKE FROM IT HERE

WRITE DOWN ANY KEY BIBLE VERSES

JOURNAL SPACE

WRITE DOWN ANY OTHER NOTES, THOUGHTS AND IDEAS FROM YOUR READINGS

RANDOM BIBLE VERSE

PRAY AND ASK GOD TO GIVE YOU A VERSE

FLIP TO A RANDOM PAGE IN YOUR BIBLE OR GOOGLE 'BIBLE DICE'

PRAYER REQUESTS

WHAT DO YOU NEED TO ASK GOD FOR TODAY?

"Anxiety weighs down the heart,

but a kind word cheers it up."

Proverbs 12:25

DAY 17/28

DATE: / /

THOUGHTS & FEELINGS

WRITE DOWN WHAT IS CURRENTLY ON YOUR MIND / HOW YOU'RE FEELING

E.G. STRESSED ABOUT WORK / THANKFUL FOR FRIENDS

PRAYER

TAKE THOSE THOUGHTS AND FEELINGS TO GOD

GOD PLEASE HELP ME...

THANK YOU GOD FOR...

READING

READ A DEVOTION OR THE BIBLE

WRITE DOWN ANY KEY PRINCIPLES THAT YOU CAN TAKE FROM IT HERE

WRITE DOWN ANY KEY BIBLE VERSES

JOURNAL SPACE

WRITE DOWN ANY OTHER NOTES, THOUGHTS AND IDEAS FROM YOUR READINGS

RANDOM BIBLE VERSE

PRAY AND ASK GOD TO GIVE YOU A VERSE

FLIP TO A RANDOM PAGE IN YOUR BIBLE OR GOOGLE 'BIBLE DICE'

PRAYER REQUESTS

WHAT DO YOU NEED TO ASK GOD FOR TODAY?

"FOR I AM CONVINCED THAT NEITHER DEATH NOR LIFE, NEITHER ANGELS NOR DEMONS, NEITHER THE PRESENT NOR THE FUTURE, NOR ANY POWERS, NEITHER HEIGHT NOR DEPTH, NOR ANYTHING ELSE IN ALL CREATION, WILL BE ABLE TO SEPARATE US FROM THE LOVE OF GOD THAT IS IN CHRIST JESUS OUR LORD."

ROMANS 8:38–39

DAY 18/28

DATE: / /

THOUGHTS & FEELINGS

WRITE DOWN WHAT IS CURRENTLY ON YOUR MIND / HOW YOU'RE FEELING

E.G. STRESSED ABOUT WORK / THANKFUL FOR FRIENDS

PRAYER

TAKE THOSE THOUGHTS AND FEELINGS TO GOD

GOD PLEASE HELP ME...

THANK YOU GOD FOR...

READING

READ A DEVOTION OR THE BIBLE

WRITE DOWN ANY KEY PRINCIPLES THAT YOU CAN TAKE FROM IT HERE

WRITE DOWN ANY KEY BIBLE VERSES

JOURNAL SPACE

WRITE DOWN ANY OTHER NOTES, THOUGHTS AND IDEAS FROM YOUR READINGS

RANDOM BIBLE VERSE

PRAY AND ASK GOD TO GIVE YOU A VERSE

FLIP TO A RANDOM PAGE IN YOUR BIBLE OR GOOGLE 'BIBLE DICE'

PRAYER REQUESTS

WHAT DO YOU NEED TO ASK GOD FOR TODAY?

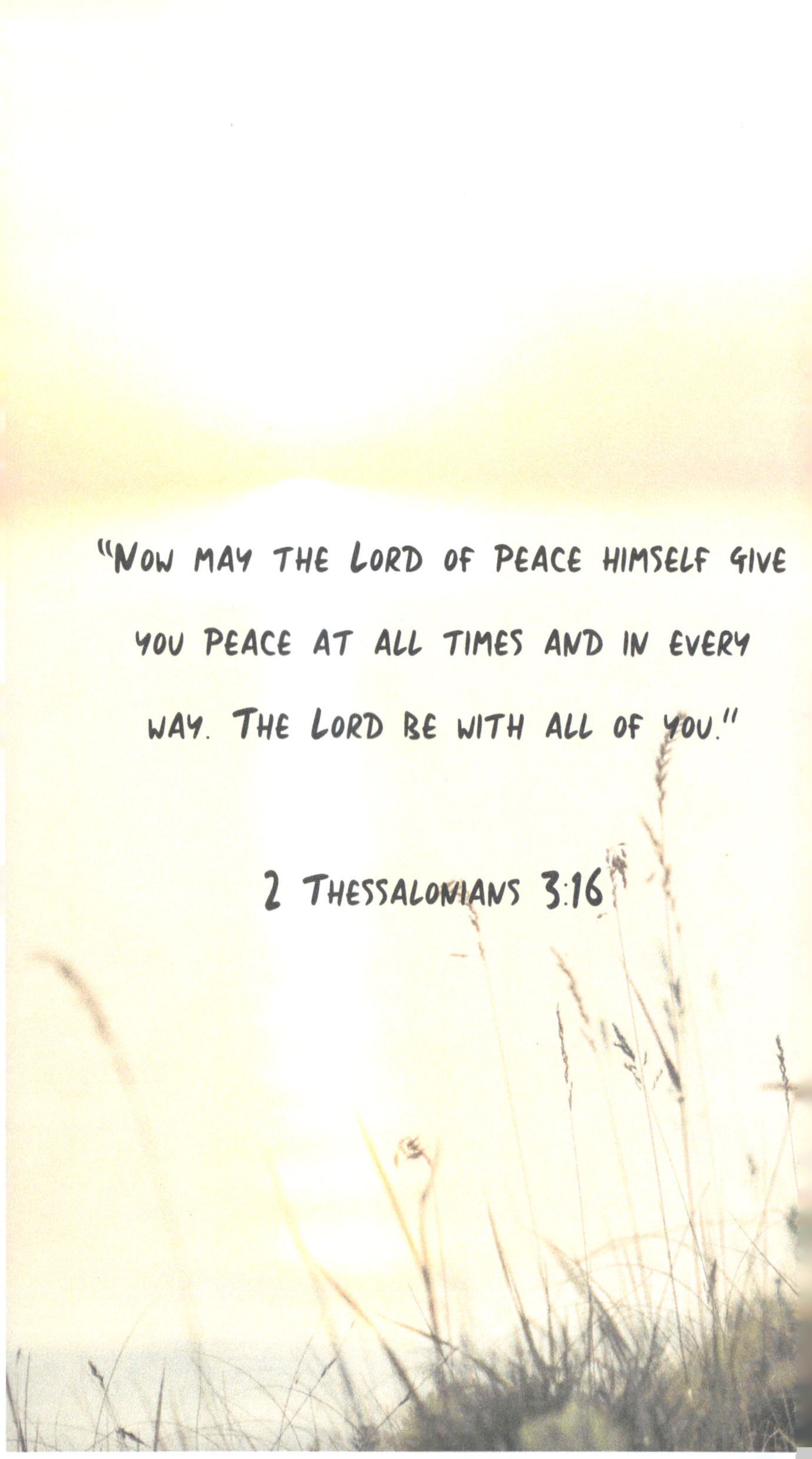
"Now may the Lord of peace himself give
you peace at all times and in every
way. The Lord be with all of you."
2 Thessalonians 3:16

DAY 19/28

DATE: / /

THOUGHTS & FEELINGS

WRITE DOWN WHAT IS CURRENTLY ON YOUR MIND / HOW YOU'RE FEELING

E.G. STRESSED ABOUT WORK / THANKFUL FOR FRIENDS

PRAYER

TAKE THOSE THOUGHTS AND FEELINGS TO GOD

GOD PLEASE HELP ME...

THANK YOU GOD FOR...

READING

READ A DEVOTION OR THE BIBLE

WRITE DOWN ANY KEY PRINCIPLES THAT YOU CAN TAKE FROM IT HERE

WRITE DOWN ANY KEY BIBLE VERSES

JOURNAL SPACE

WRITE DOWN ANY OTHER NOTES, THOUGHTS AND IDEAS FROM YOUR READINGS

RANDOM BIBLE VERSE

PRAY AND ASK GOD TO GIVE YOU A VERSE

FLIP TO A RANDOM PAGE IN YOUR BIBLE OR GOOGLE 'BIBLE DICE'

PRAYER REQUESTS

WHAT DO YOU NEED TO ASK GOD FOR TODAY?

"Do not conform to the pattern of this world, but be transformed by the renewing of your mind. Then you will be able to test and approve what God's will is—his good, pleasing and perfect will."

Romans 12:2

DAY 20/28

DATE: / /

THOUGHTS & FEELINGS

WRITE DOWN WHAT IS CURRENTLY ON YOUR MIND / HOW YOU'RE FEELING

E.G. STRESSED ABOUT WORK / THANKFUL FOR FRIENDS

PRAYER

TAKE THOSE THOUGHTS AND FEELINGS TO GOD

GOD PLEASE HELP ME...

THANK YOU GOD FOR...

READING

READ A DEVOTION OR THE BIBLE

WRITE DOWN ANY KEY PRINCIPLES THAT YOU CAN TAKE FROM IT HERE

WRITE DOWN ANY KEY BIBLE VERSES

JOURNAL SPACE

WRITE DOWN ANY OTHER NOTES, THOUGHTS AND IDEAS FROM YOUR READINGS

RANDOM BIBLE VERSE

PRAY AND ASK GOD TO GIVE YOU A VERSE

FLIP TO A RANDOM PAGE IN YOUR BIBLE OR GOOGLE 'BIBLE DICE'

PRAYER REQUESTS

WHAT DO YOU NEED TO ASK GOD FOR TODAY?

"WHEN ANXIETY WAS GREAT WITHIN ME,

YOUR CONSOLATION BROUGHT ME JOY."

PSALM 94:19

DAY 21/28

DATE: / /

THOUGHTS & FEELINGS

WRITE DOWN WHAT IS CURRENTLY ON YOUR MIND / HOW YOU'RE FEELING

E.G. STRESSED ABOUT WORK / THANKFUL FOR FRIENDS

PRAYER

TAKE THOSE THOUGHTS AND FEELINGS TO GOD

GOD PLEASE HELP ME...

THANK YOU GOD FOR...

READING

READ A DEVOTION OR THE BIBLE

WRITE DOWN ANY KEY PRINCIPLES THAT YOU CAN TAKE FROM IT HERE

WRITE DOWN ANY KEY BIBLE VERSES

JOURNAL SPACE

WRITE DOWN ANY OTHER NOTES, THOUGHTS AND IDEAS FROM YOUR READINGS

RANDOM BIBLE VERSE

PRAY AND ASK GOD TO GIVE YOU A VERSE

FLIP TO A RANDOM PAGE IN YOUR BIBLE OR GOOGLE 'BIBLE DICE'

PRAYER REQUESTS

WHAT DO YOU NEED TO ASK GOD FOR TODAY?

"Humble yourselves, therefore, under God's mighty hand, that he may lift you up in due time. Cast all your anxiety on him because he cares for you."

1 Peter 5:6–7

DAY 22/28

DATE: / /

THOUGHTS & FEELINGS

WRITE DOWN WHAT IS CURRENTLY ON YOUR MIND / HOW YOU'RE FEELING

E.G. STRESSED ABOUT WORK / THANKFUL FOR FRIENDS

PRAYER

TAKE THOSE THOUGHTS AND FEELINGS TO GOD

GOD PLEASE HELP ME...

THANK YOU GOD FOR...

READING

READ A DEVOTION OR THE BIBLE

WRITE DOWN ANY KEY PRINCIPLES THAT YOU CAN TAKE FROM IT HERE

WRITE DOWN ANY KEY BIBLE VERSES

JOURNAL SPACE

WRITE DOWN ANY OTHER NOTES, THOUGHTS AND IDEAS FROM YOUR READINGS

RANDOM BIBLE VERSE

PRAY AND ASK GOD TO GIVE YOU A VERSE

FLIP TO A RANDOM PAGE IN YOUR BIBLE OR GOOGLE 'BIBLE DICE'

PRAYER REQUESTS

WHAT DO YOU NEED TO ASK GOD FOR TODAY?

"He will wipe every tear from their eyes. There will be no more death or mourning or crying or pain, for the old order of things has passed away."

Revelation 21:4

DAY 23/28

DATE: / /

THOUGHTS & FEELINGS

WRITE DOWN WHAT IS CURRENTLY ON YOUR MIND / HOW YOU'RE FEELING

E.G. STRESSED ABOUT WORK / THANKFUL FOR FRIENDS

PRAYER

TAKE THOSE THOUGHTS AND FEELINGS TO GOD

GOD PLEASE HELP ME...

THANK YOU GOD FOR...

READING

READ A DEVOTION OR THE BIBLE

WRITE DOWN ANY KEY PRINCIPLES THAT YOU CAN TAKE FROM IT HERE

WRITE DOWN ANY KEY BIBLE VERSES

JOURNAL SPACE

WRITE DOWN ANY OTHER NOTES, THOUGHTS AND IDEAS FROM YOUR READINGS

RANDOM BIBLE VERSE

PRAY AND ASK GOD TO GIVE YOU A VERSE

FLIP TO A RANDOM PAGE IN YOUR BIBLE OR GOOGLE 'BIBLE DICE'

PRAYER REQUESTS

WHAT DO YOU NEED TO ASK GOD FOR TODAY?

"Now to him who is able to do immeasurably more than all we ask or imagine, according to his power that is at work within us."

Ephesians 3:20

DAY 24/28 DATE: / /

THOUGHTS & FEELINGS

WRITE DOWN WHAT IS CURRENTLY ON YOUR MIND / HOW YOU'RE FEELING

E.G. STRESSED ABOUT WORK / THANKFUL FOR FRIENDS

PRAYER

TAKE THOSE THOUGHTS AND FEELINGS TO GOD

GOD PLEASE HELP ME...

THANK YOU GOD FOR...

READING

READ A DEVOTION OR THE BIBLE

WRITE DOWN ANY KEY PRINCIPLES THAT YOU CAN TAKE FROM IT HERE

WRITE DOWN ANY KEY BIBLE VERSES

JOURNAL SPACE

WRITE DOWN ANY OTHER NOTES, THOUGHTS AND IDEAS FROM YOUR READINGS

RANDOM BIBLE VERSE

PRAY AND ASK GOD TO GIVE YOU A VERSE

FLIP TO A RANDOM PAGE IN YOUR BIBLE OR GOOGLE 'BIBLE DICE'

PRAYER REQUESTS

WHAT DO YOU NEED TO ASK GOD FOR TODAY?

"Blessed be God— he heard me praying. He proved he's on my side; I've thrown my lot in with him. Now I'm jumping for joy, and shouting and singing my thanks to him."

Psalm 28:7

DAY 25/28

DATE: / /

THOUGHTS & FEELINGS

WRITE DOWN WHAT IS CURRENTLY ON YOUR MIND / HOW YOU'RE FEELING

E.G. STRESSED ABOUT WORK / THANKFUL FOR FRIENDS

PRAYER

TAKE THOSE THOUGHTS AND FEELINGS TO GOD

GOD PLEASE HELP ME...

THANK YOU GOD FOR...

READING

READ A DEVOTION OR THE BIBLE

WRITE DOWN ANY KEY PRINCIPLES THAT YOU CAN TAKE FROM IT HERE

WRITE DOWN ANY KEY BIBLE VERSES

JOURNAL SPACE

WRITE DOWN ANY OTHER NOTES, THOUGHTS AND IDEAS FROM YOUR READING

RANDOM BIBLE VERSE

PRAY AND ASK GOD TO GIVE YOU A VERSE

FLIP TO A RANDOM PAGE IN YOUR BIBLE OR GOOGLE 'BIBLE DICE'

PRAYER REQUESTS

WHAT DO YOU NEED TO ASK GOD FOR TODAY?

"But grow in the grace and knowledge of our Lord and Savior Jesus Christ. To him be glory both now and forever! Amen."

2 Peter 3:18

DAY 26/28

DATE: / /

THOUGHTS & FEELINGS

WRITE DOWN WHAT IS CURRENTLY ON YOUR MIND / HOW YOU'RE FEELING

E.G. STRESSED ABOUT WORK / THANKFUL FOR FRIENDS

PRAYER

TAKE THOSE THOUGHTS AND FEELINGS TO GOD

GOD PLEASE HELP ME...

THANK YOU GOD FOR...

READING

READ A DEVOTION OR THE BIBLE

WRITE DOWN ANY KEY PRINCIPLES THAT YOU CAN TAKE FROM IT HERE

WRITE DOWN ANY KEY BIBLE VERSES

JOURNAL SPACE

WRITE DOWN ANY OTHER NOTES, THOUGHTS AND IDEAS FROM YOUR READINGS

RANDOM BIBLE VERSE

PRAY AND ASK GOD TO GIVE YOU A VERSE

FLIP TO A RANDOM PAGE IN YOUR BIBLE OR GOOGLE 'BIBLE DICE'

PRAYER REQUESTS

WHAT DO YOU NEED TO ASK GOD FOR TODAY?

"FOR NOTHING WILL BE IMPOSSIBLE WITH GOD."

LUKE 1:37

DAY 27/28

DATE: / /

THOUGHTS & FEELINGS

WRITE DOWN WHAT IS CURRENTLY ON YOUR MIND / HOW YOU'RE FEELING

E.G. STRESSED ABOUT WORK / THANKFUL FOR FRIENDS

PRAYER

TAKE THOSE THOUGHTS AND FEELINGS TO GOD

GOD PLEASE HELP ME...

THANK YOU GOD FOR...

READING

READ A DEVOTION OR THE BIBLE

WRITE DOWN ANY KEY PRINCIPLES THAT YOU CAN TAKE FROM IT HERE

WRITE DOWN ANY KEY BIBLE VERSES

JOURNAL SPACE

WRITE DOWN ANY OTHER NOTES, THOUGHTS AND IDEAS FROM YOUR READING:

RANDOM BIBLE VERSE

PRAY AND ASK GOD TO GIVE YOU A VERSE

FLIP TO A RANDOM PAGE IN YOUR BIBLE OR GOOGLE 'BIBLE DICE'

PRAYER REQUESTS

WHAT DO YOU NEED TO ASK GOD FOR TODAY?

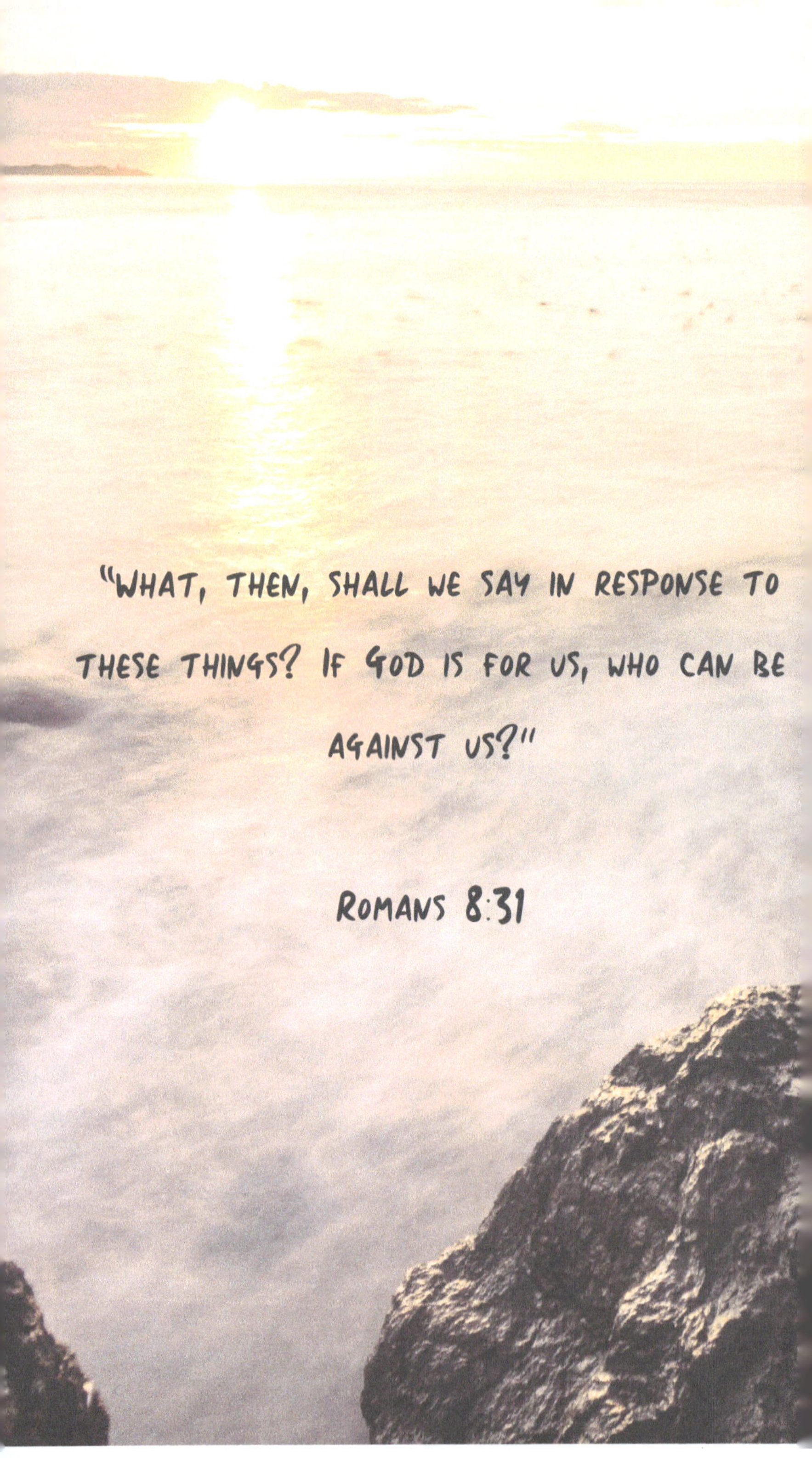
"WHAT, THEN, SHALL WE SAY IN RESPONSE TO THESE THINGS? IF GOD IS FOR US, WHO CAN BE AGAINST US?"
ROMANS 8:31

DAY 28/28

DATE: / /

THOUGHTS & FEELINGS

WRITE DOWN WHAT IS CURRENTLY ON YOUR MIND / HOW YOU'RE FEELING

E.G. STRESSED ABOUT WORK / THANKFUL FOR FRIENDS

PRAYER

TAKE THOSE THOUGHTS AND FEELINGS TO GOD

GOD PLEASE HELP ME...

THANK YOU GOD FOR...

READING

READ A DEVOTION OR THE BIBLE

WRITE DOWN ANY KEY PRINCIPLES THAT YOU CAN TAKE FROM IT HERE

WRITE DOWN ANY KEY BIBLE VERSES

JOURNAL SPACE

WRITE DOWN ANY OTHER NOTES, THOUGHTS AND IDEAS FROM YOUR READINGS

RANDOM BIBLE VERSE

PRAY AND ASK GOD TO GIVE YOU A VERSE

FLIP TO A RANDOM PAGE IN YOUR BIBLE OR GOOGLE 'BIBLE DICE'

PRAYER REQUESTS

WHAT DO YOU NEED TO ASK GOD FOR TODAY?

YOU'VE MADE IT!

CONGRATS! YOU'VE SPENT ANOTHER 28 DAYS WITH GOD.

GO BACK TO THE BEGINNING OF THIS SECTION AND REVISIT YOUR STRUGGLES AND BREAKTHROUGHS.

ONCE YOU'RE DONE, COMPLETE THE GUIDED REFLECTION.

REFLECTION

REFLECT ON THE PAST 28 DAYS. WHAT HAS GOD TAUGHT OR SHOWN YOU?

How have you seen God work in your three areas of need?

THOUGH OUR CIRCUMSTANCES MAY CHANGE, THE GOODNESS OF GOD REMAINS THE SAME.

GOD HAS INCREDIBLE PLANS FOR YOUR LIFE! NOT ONLY DOES HE WANT TO TAKE YOU TO YOUR PLACE OF PURPOSE, HE PROMISES TO GUIDE YOU ALONG THE WAY.

PSALM 32:8:

"I WILL GUIDE YOU ALONG THE BEST PATHWAY FOR YOUR LIFE. I WILL ADVISE YOU AND WATCH OVER YOU."

IT IS ONLY WHEN WE SPEND TIME WITH GOD, THAT HE CAN REVEAL HIS PERFECT PLANS. PUT HIM FIRST, AND HE'LL GUIDE YOU TO AN UNBELIEVABLE FUTURE.

WE ENCOURAGE YOU TO CONTINUE TO DOCUMENT YOUR JOURNEY WITH GOD. KEEP THIS JOURNAL AND REVISIT IT OFTEN, AS A REMINDER OF HIS INCREDIBLE PROVISION IN YOUR LIFE.

"The faithful love of the Lord never ends! His mercies never cease. Great is his faithfulness; his mercies begin afresh each morning."

Lamentations 3:22–23

Ark House Press
arkhousepress.com

Cataloguing in Publication Data:
Title: Cancel Your Plans I've Got Something Better: 28 Day Journal
ISBN: 978-0-6456705-6-1 (pbk)
Subjects: REL012150 [RELIGION / Christian Living / Devotional Journal]; REL012070 [RELIGION / Christian Living / Personal Growth];
Other Authors/Contributors: Young, Christy;

CPSIA information can be obtained
at www.ICGtesting.com
Printed in the USA
LVHW072259220323
742311LV00001B/2

* 9 7 8 0 6 4 5 6 7 0 5 6 1 *